GW00492798

# LOVE
# DEATH
# AND
# OTHER
# JOYS

**Other Poetry by Bernard Kops**

Poems and Songs (Scorpion Press) 1958
An Anemone for Antigone (Scorpion Press) 1959
Erica, I Want To Read You Something (Scorpion Press) 1967
For the Record (Secker and Warburg) 1971
Barricades in West Hampstead (Hearing Eye) 1988
Grandchildren and Other Poems (Hearing Eye) 2000
Where Do People Go (The Happy Dragons Press) 2004
This Room in the Sunlight: Collected Poems (David Paul) 2010

# LOVE
# DEATH
# AND
# OTHER
# JOYS

**Bernard Kops**

DAVID
PAUL

First published in Great Britain in 2018
By David Paul
25 Methuen Park
London N10 2JR


www.davidpaulbooks.com

ISBN 9780954054298


Printed in Great Britain

For Erica

# Contents

# Love Song for Erica in the Ocean of Forever

How beautiful the slow distancing;
the journey of this life, exchanged
for the longer journey of the longing heart.
Oh! There is no loss in this dissolving
planet of life.
Our grandchildren's laughter, our waves
lingering forever around us on this raft of
longing and belonging.
The shooting stars, their showers
feed our hearts, our silhouettes.
Flowers of eternity cover the walls
and our roof shelters us from the cosmic wind.
So, you and I and our love lives forever.
And for always.

# Morning Song for my Ninety First Year

Morning opens my eyes and it is Monday,
five twenty a.m.
And I have just come from my dream
and my waking when the mouth of my earth comes
through with these words.
Where the morning of sunlight creeps through the
windows of light, sight and the darkness flying of the
night.
I sing as I work. For work is the passion,
the panacea of being.
And joy is for living, and the miracle of breathing.
Therefore life is for everyone and her name is Erica.
Where at this lasting moment she happens to like
sleeping with my heart and her loving, and her moment
murmuring, for her journey beside me,
as she sings her songs of the universe,
with the warmth of her body.
And my heart pounding the songs of our being.
Out of her sleeping, our last great-great granddaughter,
Mishmish, our Apricot cat for all seasons comes rushing,
seeking world outside.

Miow and miowing as she mumbles goodbye, and flies
through the cat-flap, diving into garden,
where earth and Daffodils and Bluebells are also
breathing and dancing;
and singing the songs of today and tomorrow.

# Erica Asleep

In this room of space,
beneath a myriad of stars,
Erica is fast asleep, under
the canopy of the dreams
of life.
Nothing else happens,
Except she is there;
breathing in the silence
and the smell of earth.
I whisper.
Love of my life. Life of my love.
See you in the morning.

## Erica Rises

Your halo heat
lay in bed beside me
and around me
when you got up.
And the singing,
moaning wind
of winter laughed
through the trees,
singing lullabies
that made me
slowly dance through
the dark
for the rest of the day.

## The Sun and the Moon

In the morning of our lives,
the sun waves burst
through the back window,
where the garden lurks.
It's early morning when birds
declare the day
and the clouds decide
to slink away.
In the day, in the glow
of late life,
when we weave our memories
and pour golden light
upon laughter and the
tears, on the skein of our years.
And the sun, arching, wanders
through window glass,
gazing upon us
until it is late afternoon.
And it all goes too quickly
and too soon.
And the streets sleep
and snore.

And the moon creeps
on her cold lonely journey
across the molten sky
and the sun seeps
into the cracks in the pavements
and so do I.

## The Swifts

The swifts are swooping over
the communal garden at five
in the morning.
You would have seen them
if you were as early, and as mad as me.
With my face pressed at glass and staring
through the window.
And the trees and the clouds
and the sky and the smell of grass.
How beautiful they were, those birds.
Swooping and diving and soaring;
their beaks working and swallowing,
then turning. All in the sky.
And I wanted to cry as they swept away.
They didn't hear me as I softly shouted:
Goodbye! Goodbye!

# The Floating Away

The golden waves are taking me
far away, far away.
Dear wife; my dear enchanting love;
dear aeons of my children. Do not cry.
For my tears do not tear me.
They are merely angels, so laugh with them
as they dive into the forever sea.
Dear family strangers, those who still survive
the frenzied mouth of death.
You will never be lost to me,
as I swim through the dreams of existence.
You have come through the cauldron of birth
and I, in my journey, will sing our songs.

# Two A.M.

I thought I belonged to mother earth.
From love and song and trees and sky
and night and day and work and play
and was I here? And who was I?
From family and joy then I must go.
And when and where I do not know.
And from she who gave me every day.

For now I see those faces gone.
Familiars gone from this world of light.
They float towards me, call my name
and beckon me to endless night.

How very sad I cannot stay.
But more and more I am called away.

## Mayday 2016

Gone are the fascists on this glorious day
and the stench of politicians.
Gone is the madness of the world,
for this is the first of May.
Gone are the turbines of industry
and the noise of swallow traffic,
pouring the screaming mad
into the roads to nowhere.
And Erica and I are in the garden
gathering the harvest of sunshine.

# Kafka Laughed

We were walking towards the horizon
when he started to sing.
"Look, the Hills! From whence cometh no help."
"Where are we going?" I cried. "And who are you
And why are you smiling?"
He laughed.
"And where is my family? My wife, my love, my life?"
He marched on, faster and faster;
laughing again and again; nodding at me
to enjoy.
"I don't understand. Where are the people I loved?
My tears dropped into the sand. He sang again.
I sat down where there was nothing and no-one.
"Who are you? Where are we going?" I shouted.
"Worry not dear boy. Death is fine, it's certainty,
it's certainly not as ridiculous as life."
I tried to remember my wife; her smile, her flesh,
her beauty.
I closed my eyes.
He hugged me.

"Who are you?" I said softly.
He put his strong arms around me.
And hugged and hugged me.
"I'm Franz Kafka." He laughed and the mountains
were in his eyes.
"And I have left behind all my children,
all my photographs."
"We are almost there. Look!"
He jumped up and down; like a child.
"But we may never get there," I cried.
And I walked and walked with him,
slowly, slowly.
And Kafka laughed and laughed.

# Waiting for the Barbarians

I feel so alone, so I close my eyes
and sing inside your words, remembering you were
one of the greatest poets in the world.
Dying in 1933, just when the Harbinger of destruction,
the angel of death, was born.
But you never really died. Cavafy! Your words live on.
Yes! Truly these are bad times.
But you sleep. You are gone. So sleep on,
in your Grecian cemetery.
Your words, your songs still stir me.
Maybe they can still steer our world away
from madness.
I speak a line from one of your best poems.
Not your Ithica, your words of joy.
But your prophecy.
The fearsome, chilling, threnody.
The Barbarians Are Coming.
In the darkness of my bed, I fear your foresight.
Sleep on, sleep on, oh marvellous poet.
It is for us who are still alive to awake.

And wake the world.

# Black Cherries of Midnight

Look!
There is a bowl of black cherries
on the table.
Let's stuff ourselves
with the dark syrup of love.
And sleep. And sleep.

# Four Trees In My Garden

My long dead mother was calling me
when I went out, sleepwalking
into the garden.
I looked up into the dark blue sky
where Garcia Lorca was looking down
from the sharp corner of the moon.
Go to the trees and smell the leaves
he sang to me.
There are four trees in my garden.
So I found myself under the olive tree,
taking the leaves into my hands
and the aroma bursting me away, away,
where far dead soldiers were singing.
*Viva La Quinta Brigada. Rumba la,*
*Rumba la, rumba la. Ay Carmela!*
*Ay Carmela!*
I lift my heart soaring
towards my mulberry tree.
And to the Hebrew leaf I rubbed
into my face. And a voice far
off, from Galilee, danced with a soft breeze
towards all the trees.

*Yesh li gan ulvayesh li*
I have a garden and in it is a well.

And so I went to the myrtle bush
where my mother sang from the ghost past.
"Go to sleep my baby, close you pretty blue eyes.
Angels are above peeping down upon you
From the skies." Then into her Yiddish.
Rozhinkes mit mandlen, schluff my kindele, schluff.
Almonds and raisins! The bitter and the sweet.
The story of Jewish life.
I walked towards the open door
where stood my Mimosa tree.
Plucking a leaf and a mimosa flower,
I cried. Then went inside
where my mother softly sang
and disappeared into the mirror.
I took my one leaf and flower then whispered:
enclose me mimosa with your smell of almonds.
Let me die with my eyes full of flowers.

## Mother

A wife is a wife, Chekov said.
My mother was a wife, and what a wife,
and what a mother.
A mother and a half.
Soft and fat and beautiful;
cuddling all of us together. An octopus,
enfolding with her tentacles.
I loved the smell of her. I drowned myself
deep into her stained and ancient cloth,
into the beautiful dark of her years,
years of all her ages.
Her tears always ready, forming
in her eyes, encircling days and nights.
A flowing river of hope
and fears for tomorrow.
Stroking and smiling and mumbling
unknown morning lullabies.
These were all her words in her world.
And she would dance in the bedrooms
with all seven of us.
But soon enough her smile would fade
and she would sigh. And sigh.

God is good, she always said,
in the morning and the night when
we went to bed.
But soon the war came and went.
Our cuddling and dancing and singing
was over. But she never cried.
Her tears went hard and stuck in her eyes.
She came out of cuddling and out of sunshine,
for everything had gone up in smoke.
After that no-one spoke.
And all the Jewish mothers left in the world
stared into space.
"So what about God? Where was he?
And where is he now?"I shouted and I cried.
"The answer is there is no answer." She smiled and
replied.
Then she went shtumm and into her bedroom,
where she prayed to her God
that was never there.
And after that she died. My mother!
The Mother of the world!
And soon the home folded
and I slipped away.

# Father

My father fell from the dark stars
and wandered in the garden of
frozen dreams. He was lost
and never really found the earth.
Here he crashed into the lightning
of my mother's life
and gave her seven children to feed.
So we all carried on,
swallowing the days away, crouched
in that cradle of the universe
called Stepney Green.
My father was useless, impossible.
Broke and broken, just about surviving,
by the breath of little children.
But wait! Hang on!
One day, long after he was truly dead I remember
he suddenly stood on a chair and shouted.
"Children! Listen!
I've been given two tickets to the opera,
Aida in Bethnal Green.
Who wants to go with me?"
Silence was the loud reply.
"I'll go! I'll go!" I said. And I went and awoke.
You can never tell who holds the key.
My poor father opened the door for me.

# Erica in the Living Room

Erica in the living room.
I was in my dying room;
her humming telling me
that I had come through,
defying the tentacles of death.
Now the days flow past,
dancing through the window glass.
Monday and Friday get married
on Saturday.
The children come and play and eat
away on Sunday.
Another hurrying week of lovely nothingness.
Now the silence when the clouds
of Monday again, slowly moving
from the North to the final goal of Southwest,
darkens my day and I put away my mourning.
Soon all the faces and names I knew fall
into my memory soup. I swallow them all,
with not so many years of tears filling
my eyes.
Yet I still hear the laughter and cries
from all my children, and their children

who have drifted away
like the clouds in the skies.
Beautiful girls and boys after play.
To find and go their own way.
There is nothing more to say,
Before sleep. Except I smile in the mirror
for the only one in the living room,
who came to stay.

## Morning

Days flash past. But in the morning
we snatch a little time as they slow down.
Our eyes seek smiles from the other.
And Edvard Grieg enveloping, embracing
the world in his Morning.
Ringing, bringing song and joy.
I have tears, so I break the silence.
Are you still there? I ask.
Are you still with us? She answers.
Our laughter causes the golden yellow sunflowers
in the vase by the window to lighten the room.
I love the nothingness of time.
We live in the beauty of being.

But memory has its way and the aunts
and dead parents cry and sing, dance and scream
as they die in the clouds that slowly, slowly pass.
The years follow us and the years fly away.
A strange joy surrounds
my years that have gone
and the violin mellows.
Lost faces stare at me
from the trees.
And they laugh through their tears.
And so do I.


## A Wife is a Wife

Once she gazed upon my face with adoration.
Now she brushes my mouth for crumbs,
smoothes my shoulders, combs my hair.
So, so beautiful the way she hums.
She hands me a mirror, calls me handsome.
I see that time is not my friend.
She is my beginning, my middle
and my end.

# Walking With Peter

*In memory of Peter Mejer*

Walking with Peter
we were like children
happy and silly,
singing lost songs.
A trio of fiends
across Hampstead Heath
and in Golders Hill Park.
Erica and Peter and
me in the middle.
We dawdled together
every day we were there
talking of angels and God
not all there.
And Peter hugged trees
in Kenwood in the rain.
And we laughed in the sunshine
for this was our world
in that forest of dreams
where life was forever
and ever and ever
and no one cried.
And nobody died.

## Busride

Doors opening. Doors closing.
A long journey in a very crowded bus.
Doors opening. Doors closing.
A very long message
for a very short life.
Doors opening. Doors closing.


## Morning Appointment

I am on my way to Swiss Cottage
where the children swim in the
sun.
And in my mind I join them
And life is for everyone.
I am on my way to the doctor's
for another injection of breath,
and I poke out my tongue
and laugh and dance
in the shadow of the angel of death.

# Long Text Message

So here I am
laughing, crying and fully dead.
So, what's the big deal?
In the dying room they laughed
when I begged them.
Can I take my mobile with me?
The dead are dead, they said.
But I'm still human, I cried.
And the dying still have desires
and dreams. Worth a try.
Sure. Okay. We'll slip it in the fire with
your bones, they replied.
So here I am. And just to say
I'm sending this message
from the other side of time,
in the forlorn hope that I will find you.

I dreamed of you again last night,
a million stars ago.
I hate these lonely shores of aloneness.
If you receive this
please text me back.
Tell me you remember.

Say we were there.
Tell me it happened.
And we loved. And were loving.
Meanwhile I await. And wait!
And I shall wait forever.

## The Death Of Death

In this drab empty morning
gloomy Sunday enters, striding,
smirking into my day.
And nothing will change.
I am all dried up
with the usual fear of the
nothingness of being
that touches, clutches my fearful, dying heart.
And nothing can lift me for all is gone.
I do not believe in miracles,
or oracles to boat me away.
Here I must stay where
darkness swirls and death is forever.
And our children have come and gone,
as they must.
Life now has no meaning.
And all my tears have dried
into dust. And the man that was
is not inside.
I looked out of the back window
to drown myself in the murky sky.
And there was the one rose on
a dying stem, in the November
of my years.

And it opened, the rose, and so did the clouds
and the sky mellowed,
separating my world from winter.
A beautiful woman opened the door.
And I opened my eyes and the dark ascended.
She was, she is, my wife,
who brought the world out of night into light.
With a cup of coffee and without a word
in her silver rosy necklace I saw myself smiling.
And like the only rose in winter
that morning was the death of mourning
and the death of death.

# Winter Spring Song

It is midwinter but I will close my eyes
to see the daffodils that have come, springing
and the violets and the crocus.
Thus I believe next year will arrive
Now all the dark world has fled.
Then I stoop to the vine
to feel the buds are breaking.
And tomorrow will be today
when the sun looks down,
kissing me from her throne of sky.
Soon the tumbling children
in the garden will show spring sings.
Reminding me I did not die last year.
Therefore I shall be alive, again and again.
All this joy proves that I am here.
I look up in my blindness
to see the willows have come again.
Swaying, waving at me, boasting
they are the first on the communal green.
All the other trees stretch and moan,
gradually opening their yawning leaves
for blue tits to dart from tree to tree.
So I open my eyes and sing
as I walk around this winter garden,
slowly, slowly, breathing in this new thing
called life.

# Suddenly

Suddenly has always been there.
Girls have always flown out
of South Hampstead School
as if there is no time. Some are jabbering, frail.
And some are so sad. They do not smile, but
flick their locks as they walk down
into the world of Finchley Road.
Yesterday they were somewhere else.
They were children then. They were alive
when they danced in their childhood,
in their nursery land.
Suddenly they are waking and walking
into a world that is waiting to devour them.
And suddenly, there is no more suddenly.

## Two Girls

Two girls cavorting on the grass
in the rain; on the slopes
of the communal garden.
In the throes of joy, enjoying this stolen moment,
under the threatening charcoal clouds.
And no one else about.
Not a soul, only the dead,
prying through the eyes of croaking magpies.
From the slanting of sky I remember another snow;
years and years and aeons, of weeks and days
and how they come and go.
And Erica, that snapshot!
Captured our grandchildren
turning somersaults in a snowstorm
that over-coated our green. Remember?
All those sepia scenes ago?
Or so it seems. Or are they dreams?
Time flies, but where to?
And on whose wings?
But the twinning and the twining
and the turning of every season.

And the dizzy, daft maidens.
On the grass, flinging evergreen leaves
everywhere.

And the chuckling of the past years.
And the girls, falling, uncaring;
and the boys, unaware of anyone outside themselves.
Our children. Our grandchildren. Our progeny.
They glide and dance on their empty planet of youth.
Falling, catapulting, rolling down the slopes,
with the rain bucketing, on sodden grass. Yesterday!
Timeless. Lost. Joy in the living now.
Over and over they go. Then turning
somersaults in the grip of winter,
laughing like the wind.

# Granddaughters

Laughter of granddaughters in faraway rooms;
and me full of tears.
I cry so easily these days.
So beautiful they are as they grow
into women.
Now they look in mirrors and
love their reflection.

But so soon to be lost and floating away.
into their lands of pleasure and tears.
And fears.
Yet one day, sometime, they will come
and throw a kiss. But they will never stay.
They will go, they will go away.
Leaving me with all the tears in this world,
But I still have one reserve. Do I deserve
great grandchildren? So young they are,
in a world so marvellous, where dying and death
is not there, not allowed.
They wipe away my tears as they pour around
and cuddle into me their love and laughter,
bringing me back my living breath.
And I watch them play, and I am drowning in
their precious joy. And life is always
and forever, now as they rush towards me.

# A Grandfather Sings

Max! You have flown to Columbia;
on the outer limits of our world;
to seek the magic island of Forever.
Superman! You have managed to escape
this dark continent and the tenements of
our time.
Meanwhile we watch and await
your ringing baptism of fire,
remembering you will draw
the sword and the word
from the stone.
Enjoy your comrades; be joyous
in your deeds;
whilst we soak in the sun
of your distant laughter.

# I Hear Shostakovich

I hear Shostakovich.
And see ahead the Dark House of Trump.
The guns are pointing towards me,
from the fearful screaming, pissing saliva of
the madman who smiles, shooting his poison.
Dictators come and go and come and go
and kill and die; one after the other.
Look! There is another one ahead,
crawling out of the shit of nightmare.
I too am crawling towards his demented palace,
smashing the sky with my fist, shouting and crying.
I can see him laughing, with his creepers.
The eternal ghosts of nightmares, of smoke and fire,
whooping, dancing around the burning flesh.
Now we must sing and desire, and love and fight
our final battle with fearless anger and
break through the walls of the tyrant.
So that he will never rise and come again.
I must dive into my dreams and
sing as I pour and stir in the joys of living.
Then, so soon, I fall into the dust,
looking upward into the sky,
where I am laughing and crying,
breathless and sighing.
We all must stand and bury the bastard
and get on with our lives.
So now I close my eyes and just listen to the music.

# Oh! Pasty Face Woman of Harlow

Oh! Pasty face woman of Harlow.
I saw you on Television.
You yawn and shout England
For the English.
And did those feet in ancient
times walk upon our precious
land for this?
Beware! Your twisted God
hath cometh with his furnace
of fire.
Spouting, spraying
molten lava
all over this land.
Heil Herr Farago!
Where will you plant your
Auschwitz?
In Essex?

## The Day the World Died

I remember that day vividly
It stands out amongst that bungle of others
that came and flashed by.
That came and went in our long lives.
The trees outside gathered all those birds.
It was wonderful to see them back.
All those silver quick creatures
singing against the sky of black.
But then the sun burst.
A beautiful golden orange of fire.
Petals of rose and green
against the blue backcloth of day.
I got up early, feeling good.
The sun had lit up our garden
And living room. Life was good as usual.
Life was life.
You came in yawning, smiling, stretching,
breathing words,
drinking in the beauty of our world,
through the glass.
We hugged silently
And then I stopped looking at you
for I noticed that the birds had gone.
I opened the door and saw the sudden daffodils
And knew it was spring.

And the world so beautiful, so smelling of life.
And all our years had flown so wonderfully
in our sudden embrace.
We smiled and kissed and laughed
as we watched that dawn
yawn and stretch into sudden day,
like it had done every day
since we first met, all those centuries ago.
How we swayed through our years.
Endless. So fast.
Then we walked out into the street
that day when the world died.
And the world was full of people, laughing,
waving and no one cried. No crack, no screaming.
Just the laughter. When we were sucked into that vortex.
All was silent, that day when the world died.

# The Survivor

After the cremation, I crawled
far from the stench of flesh.
Blazing, pounding waves
poured not from the ovens
but down from the oceans,
from the singing sun.
Wake! Wake! Sang my mother's
last lullaby.
Go! Go! Get away! And then she died.
Thus, I realised I was still alive.
But swimming wild! Hard! Insane! Seeing nothingness.
One who had escaped the madness,
the fury of humankind.
I am a child, what do I know
about Death the Gatherer?
Therefore I slip through to the far
horizon, to another existence called life.
So was it a lifetime or centuries
that came or went? Or a dream?
Will it be? Ever? Life? Was it ever here?
I dive into the sound of everlasting water!
Silence! Suddenly the screaming has gone. Gone forever.
But now I float in the sea that is my mother.
Her death is the last song that sings me to sleep.

And when I awake my eyes open to the joy of birds
with their swooping songs of laughter.
For here is the earth and the beckoning waves
from the shore,
where I find myself on the Eastern shores of Majorca.
Here the Phoenicians came with the Jews.
And here on these sands they
created glass. And then came the mirror.
Now I look to see myself. I am bones. I have no flesh.
But the sun is my mother and feeds me.
Soon the birds swoop down and sing
to the fish that fly into my mouth
and my flesh falls on to me.
In my mirror I am human again.
Music soars, drums beat.
Children who are not there dance.
A young woman, a beautiful, miraculous
vision of a lost world slowly walks towards me, smiling.
She enters my eyes. She takes my hand and I arise.
And we walk away and away, towards the rainbow.
Where are we going? I whisper.
We are going to Ithica. She laughed.
And we shall have children and children's children.
And what will we call our new god?
Wait till we get there. She smiled and we walked on.

## Songs For a Lost God.

Fate came fishing out of that place called nowhere
and let me off his hook and hurled me down
to earth.
And there was sun and there was moon
and the stars that I drank for my dreams.
Suddenly I was alive in somewhere.
And there I heard laughter from a girl,
singing and dancing out of a crowd of clouds.
You were there and I was there
and we found and founded a family,
in a place called living.
It was a time of loving and growing
and life was forever. And laughing,
sharing apricots with loving strangers,
with children and children's children.
Space and age was our destiny.
Oh! I remember that present past
and the meaning of that house of joy.
Then just when it was, it wasn't.
And one day in the middle of the night
we noticed all our birds had flown.
So we stood up and cried and laughed
and sang songs for the lost God.

# The Roundabout

Oh! Where is the beautiful acceptance of the inevitable?
If only I could see myself smiling in a dying mirror.
They say you have lived your life.
Too soon, too soon you have to go.
I scream, I smile and close my eyes
to see the one place called living.
That beautiful state called forever
where we enjoy the dream of joy.
Oh where are the lost steps to my roundabout,
where I can be with Erica, my coalescent, my love.
I laugh now and stroke her beautiful neck
and my marvellous, jealous cat Mishmish.
She purrs back in a state of wanting.
And her eyes singing that we are all in this together.

## Lotus

In the dark avalanche of time
we are a blink in the divine eye
of mother universe;
a grain of sand in the ocean
of endlessness.

How miraculous we are.

# Fishing After Death

My net sweeps through the dark,
star-scattered sky.
And I sing.
This is a marvellous catch.
She breaks the surface,
shoots up and laughs
then swims towards me.

# Blackbird on a Myrtle Bush

It is deep winter.
I could be a steel sculpture
covered in snow.
Then out of nowhere
I hear a blackbird
deep in song,
bringing me tears.
Stealing my days, my seasons,
my years.
Where did you come from?
Where did you go?
Blackbird!
Were you ever here
on that myrtle bush
covered in snow?

## Wandering through Queen Mary's Rose Garden in Regent's Park

I know Gertrude Stein once sang
"A rose is a rose is a rose."
But have you heard that roses
have bloomed three times this year,
against all the odds? Such Chutspah!
Defying all logic and the wind and the rain
and the howling headlines.
If only I could avoid the encroaching
terrible winter.
What magic to be born again
and again and again.

## The Black Birds of Riga

Erica was staring out of the window.
And no one was about.
The trees were angry, shaking their hair,
dancing crazy winter.
"Oh! For Spring," I said. "And we will
all be born again. Please God.
If he is there." I laughed.
She turned and smiled. Her sad, soft smile.
The smile a still façade; a mask to cover
something fearful.
Shall I make coffee?
Lovely. She replied, and turned to the window.
"Have you seen them today? The birds?"
"Of course." She sighed.
"Darling there is nothing out there.
You're staring into nothing, you know."
"I know. But they were sent into nothing.
I shall always see them." She murmured.
"I shall never see them." I replied.
"Darling! Look! There they go again,
those beautiful blackbirds.
All the way, all the way from Riga.
Little Leah and Yulik.
Backwards and forwards every day."

I passed her the coffee and shortbread biscuits.
"But do you have to see them?"
She didn't answer and sat down,
but still turned to the window.
"They are in my blood and in my bones."
I could see the tears gathering in her eyes.
"They were such beautiful little kids. Leah.
Just two years old and Yulick almost five.
Smashed in Rumbula, the forest of Riga,
in the brave land of Latvia."
"But that was so long ago."
She stared back at me and cried.
"It wasn't yesterday. It was today. It is every day.
Read The Times. These terrible times."
"Sorry darling." I knelt down to kiss her.
Let's go out and breathe." I said softly.
And she smiled and stood up.
"But look. Those wild crazy trees. They know.
They are furious. Fuck! Fuck! Winter.
And there they go again. Those beautiful little blackbirds.
Back to their Riga. Goodbye! Goodbye! Little ones.
There they go. Going back again."
Then she walked to the door.
"Yes! Let's go for a walk." She said.
"You never know. Soon it will be spring again."

# Auto-Da-Fé

I left home when I was twenty,
and found myself in Asturias, Northern Spain.
It was twilight, and up above
there was a village, nursing old houses
clinging together in the dark.
As dark as death.
And the children were playing in the
little square.
How slow and beautiful it all was
when Garcia Lorca flew into my mouth.
*Cantan los ninos en la noche quieta.*
*Arroyo claro, fuente serena.*
But that changed.
The ragged houses started calling me
and singing other ancient Spanish songs.
Bernard! Bernard! Hear me! See me!
I burn! I burn! *Auto-da-fe! Auto-da-fé!* They cried.
Hear me! See me! The voices sang
the everlasting Hebrew Song.
I turned to the swaying houses
where candles flickered in the windows.
Then I remembered. It was Friday night.
And an old ragged woman came out of her door.
Shivering, I cried.

Why do you burn candles on Friday night?
Laughing, she replied. I dunno! I dunno!
We always do it. It goes back a long way.
But who knows? Who knows?
And the black stream turned to the silver moon
and bowed.
I could hear the screams, swirling,
funnelling upward into the clouds.
*Auto-da-fé! Auto-da-fé!*
*Ani Maamin. Ani Maamin.*
It haunted me all night.
And will forever.

# After the Car Crash

I shuffled along the garden path
with Isaac at my arm.
And the April day wild and beautiful
howling at the naked, shivering trees.
Now he took my hand, my grandson
And guided me through the communal
garden.

I had just emerged once again
from the dark straight path of nothingness.
Into this crazy wonderful circus called life.
So I asked Isaac if he could see
the ghost children playing hide and seek
and flying through the sighing trees.
But then he sighed, my Isaac,
in such a way, as if telling me to grow up.
I've grown up too many times, I said.
And so we sat down on a bench and he smiled.
Then he threw his hands around me;
oblivious to the ghosts and giggles and life
and death.
And slowly he stroked my hand and heart.
I love you grandpa, he said
as he gently pulled me up into the world.
And ever so slowly,
we went back into the house.

# Friday Afternoon Golders Green

Sometimes I wish I could live with blind faith.
Look! I envy those guys,
who hurry towards their synagogue
for Sabbath.
They live their days observant,
pale and fanatic in their cosy enclaves;
their certain little world of Stamford Hill
and Temple Fortune.
They live belonging.
I live longing.

# An Afternoon in the Algarve

Chloe is climbing a tree rampant with olives.
I look and wave but there's fear inside me.
She shouts down "black olives Grandpa, just for you."
Oh my God, I cry to myself and wave back.
It is a beautiful day in the Algarve, in early autumn.
With the sun pouring gold down upon us.
She's now high enough to kill herself.
How many have shattered their brains
for birds to have a banquet?
The olive tree is gently waving in the air.
I screw up my eyes,
waiting for applause from the family around.
Or screams.
They're all looking up.
Families make me feel sick.
I hate myself for allowing this.
I pretend to laugh
And shout up, "Chloe, why bother?
There are plenty of black olives in the shop."
I shout again, "careful Chloe, they may be poisonous."
I turn around and whistle,
not wanting to see our beautiful lithe girl
smashed to smithereens.
There is sudden cheering

"Marvellous, she's done it, she's coming down."
I almost cry with joy.
Tears come into my eyes.
I whisper ,"Oh my God, she's won the day,"
"Wonderful Chloe. Well done. Let's go home."
Getting in the car, she looks up at me.
There is no triumphant smile on her face.
I believe she could see the aura of my desperation.
"Are you alright now Grandpa?"
I nod. She smiles slowly, knowingly.

# Jessica on the Edge

The early was late in coming
as I swam through my tears.
It was such a dark day
That didn't go away.
All through that night
I could hear the death of time.
It was my granddaughter in deep sleep.
Lying so still, so silently, trying to stay.
For in life she lived and loved,
so happily, only yesterday.
In life she, the very last person
who would ever want to get away.
Now, so far, too still.
Lost, like white marble.
Look! I say softly. Such terrible silence.
I looked for breath where she lay.
I cry for God; but he was not around
that day.
And life is a cow, without milk or eyes.
So I scream for the poor bastard in the skies.
Come back! Come back! Come back!
We all cried together, quietly within.
Please come back.

In the morning the night flew away
as the streets came alive.

Then we closed our eyes, looking upward
to the skies, knowing the dying was over.
Her face no longer marble, but alive.
And gone was all our crying.

## Alzheimer Poet

A poet only has words.
Once a poet enters... enters nowhere
he loses ... he loses ...
his words.
Look down!
Nowhere is down.
Nowhere is a strange place
where we are all destined.
Straighten your back, she says.
Straighten. Back.
She, the only one.
Never look back.
Look! Take my arm.
It is safety, it is love.
A poet enters ...
loses his ... words.
Love hangs on.
It will not let you go
to why?
It cannot be shaken off.
Shaken. Love.
I heard it once.
That's better she says.
That's much better.

The sun passes through my head.
Nowhere is now, is down.
Down is.
A poet sees the crack
in the pavement
into ...
Avert your eyes, oh ye
who enter ...
Where?
Oh God! Gone! Lost!
For always.
A poet walks into nowhere.
A poet walks.
Once a poet walks into silence.
Into ...

## Afternoon Nap

I forget the names of faces.
Friends who were there
now slouch in dark corners.
Unwrap and moan.
They watch me spooning soup
and shake their heads, laughing,
derisive.
As if I have deserted them.
I know your voices
but what are your names?
Go back to the earth.
Phoenix in the flames.
They call, the bastards.
Why do you hang on?
Names of so many, gone.
The morning's gone. And us.
They croak, Gone forever.
Welcome, they sing, come to us.
Come and live with us,
They laugh together.
They dance, they writhe.
It's time. It's time.
You can't love forever.

Tired I am,
And almost want to join the dance.
But the kids arrive!
And she, the unchanging Modigliani,
my anima, manages
to child my padded mad moods.
And jokes that pull me back together.
And answer the phone.
And the clock winds me down
And the couch sings me lullabies.
Have your afternoon nap, she
sings. And the couch nods and wafts me
lullabies. Bedibyes for tired bones.
I am wafted wonderful nothingess.
And I wake, when the clock calls time.
I leap into world and they have all gone
Those I think I once knew.
And the nothingness they try to bring.
And I dance with the kids and laugh at everything
Oh wife. Oh Life, of thee I sing.

# Hold My Arm

Remember when snow was confetti
And we agreed, laughing and running
That this was the way to go;
Somewhere we have never gone before.
Hold my arm, clutch into me.

I shall pull you into me,
So that we evaporate into each other.
Just look at this world.
The beauty came into us, out of us.
In sleep you can dream.
But not in your long sleep.
Pull over us the dark blanket of desire.
Death is yawning; laughing.
He thinks it is all for him and we are all washed up.
And we are, dancing on the long shore of love.

He always needs an adversary.

## For Sarah Musgrove

*A poem on her departure*

Down the green slide
I ride. I ride
into the fields of yesterday.
The oblique golden hills echo your name.
Come back to us tomorrow
When the whole world was joy.
And being, being.
And only love enfolds us
in her wonderful madness.


## To an Old Friend

The rosebush you gave me
when friendship was true,
growing in my garden,
still remembers you.
As for me?

Toodle-oo!

## The Communal Garden

My grandchildren on the other side
laugh with neighbours I hate.
All I can do is sit here
and pretend to read and wait.
But is my time quite long enough
for them to cross the grass
and wave and smile and dance for me
until all my angers pass.


## Michael Kustow

He's gone! Just like that.
He's gone through the door
of evermore.
Michael! Nevermore.
Now you are just a name.
And you will never come again
into this dream called life.
I look up at the night sky
where you are nothing
but fire and cloud.
I cannot cry, not aloud.
Not allowed.

# Waking

I wake, bringing another day.
The love of life and the
joy of living and the hope
of today.
And the fear of tomorrow.
And the pain of the world.
I think I shall go back to sleep.

# Night Thoughts

I have no choice; for time has lost its meaning.
I carry my death around with me.
He is a lame but jovial fellow
and one day soon with gentle courtesy
he will open the back door
and let the howling wind pour into me.
Then smiling gently he will take my fingers
and guide me away, away
from those I love.
Then humming and smiling he will pull me
into the frozen garden,
where he will smash my head
against the willow tree,
and turn me into ice confetti.

## When Marc Chagall Popped in For Breakfast

When I was a boy of five and a half
I looked out at the world
and laughed and laughed.
On that seventh floor of my dreams.
When the world went mad
and split at the seams.
And Chagall came for breakfast.
He brought doughnuts
and a cow or two
and pie in the sky
and fishes to fry.
The clouds clapped hands and trumpets danced
and my mother cried and waved at God.
And life is forever she laughed, she cried.
And my father, that poor old sod
turned to the wall and sighed and sighed.
And life the liar danced with his bride.
And all my sisters tried and tried
to sing for him and pump his pride.
He turned to the wall and scythed and sighed.
My darlings he said there is nowhere
and nothing to hide.
My mother giggled and cuddled and coddled
and sang us to sleep and wobbled like jelly.

And all the kids fell out of her belly,
and all the fishes were fried.
When Chagall waved and flew out of the door
I somehow knew there was something more,
so I went upstairs and down into bed.
But the very next morning I crept
out of the door and entered the clouds
inside my head.
And laughed all the way, away
from the beautiful suburbs of the dead.

# The Pomegranate Tree

Early this morning,
that was still yawning,
I went into the snowy garden
and plucked three ripe
pomegranates for lunch.
My offering for the love
of our life.
We devoured them together
with laughter.
Oh the sweetness in a dead land,
making music with flaming crimson
dripping from our kiss.
Later, when it was night,
I wandered back into the freezing dark.
All the leaves drooping on the bare branches.
Her frosty mouth called me. "It is winter
and the sun is dying. Did you enjoy my fruit?"
"Yes! But tell me, how can pomegranates grow
in this dead land?"

## Checkout

Standing in the queue at Waitrose,
thinking about the everlasting shores of endless space,
I feel sick with the mystery of life and the impossible
enormity
of it all.
In front of me two lovers melt into each other, oblivious.
They laugh, they kiss.
How beautiful. How wonderful. So close.
Turn out all the lights and close your eyes
as you edge closer and closer to the checkout.

## Sixty Years Married

Early morning. I awake.
Outside it is flaming June.
I must laugh and wave back
at the trees waving wildly at me.
Is it good news or bad news?
No news I can deal with.
And the rain, and the rain, and the rain,
pouring down God's tears.
I enter the joy of morning
where nothing happens,
except the heart still beating.
Therefore I am still alive.
Now my wife, my Goddess, wakes,
smiles her beauty and throws
her face at me, opening up the calming
part of the day before people come.
"Breakfast!" she sings. "Toast?"
And no one else about; no one else.
Later, the bliss of coffee.
"No! No news!" She cries.
"Turn up the music."

I bow to her smiling command
and I stretch my arms and yawn,
glad that nothing, nothing else happens,
except she laughs at my tears.
I am silent and serene as I open the door
and breathe in the garden.


## Downing Street Dirge

The poet dies,
his poetry lives on.
The soldier dies,
his gravestone lives on.
The musician dies,
his music lives on.
The politician dies,
the lies live on.

## Alzheimer Wind

It was an Alzheimer wind that lost its way.
I want to help you, what can I say?
Where did you come from and where do you go?

It grabbed my arm; its eyes drooped low.
It howled and growled, stumbled and cried.

"I come from Hell, where you will go.
And there you'll catch the dread disease
and live alone in the dark house of bees
who'll drink your blood and fill your head
with Alzheimer wind for your years ahead."

## Being Ninety

Sometimes, when I lose my balance
and fall in the street.
Strangers rush towards me.
Embarrassed, I smile. I'm fine, I say.
Thank you. And they melt away.
Back into the crowd I go on my way,
shaken, still smiling.
No wonder I believe in the deep
goodness of people.
Deep down, however hard our journey
we seem to have an instinct, for caring,
for loving each other.

# Awake and Sing

I crawl out of bed from a night that stings.
In the kitchen Erica sings.
I creep to the living room with all my things.
She comes with coffee and still she sings.
She puts on my shoes and ties the strings.
Oh my love; the joy she brings.
Throughout the house her laughter rings.
Outside in the garden the day takes wings.

## Life Where We Are Planted

As usual nothing to report
Except chaos.
If I wasn't mad,
no doubt you would drive me there.
So come into my open arms.
There are no turnings back,
no barriers to separate,
no spies,
no close friends,
no hungry wolves to feed off you.
Come, come into the cul-de-sac of dreams.
We have a shooting star that explodes.
Nothing else exists. Except love.
So embrace.
And live the day.
And night like tomorrow
never comes.

# The Third Age

I remember when I was an old man
I harangued the clouds.
I was quite irascible and growled.
I thwacked passers-by
with my walking stick.
I cursed down cul-de-sacs.
When boys kicked a ball too close,
I rushed to get there first,
to puncture it with my false teeth.
And thus I journeyed all the way to Lethe,
knowing I was unloved, unloving.
But I did not cross the river because
there was nothing on the other side.
And so I wandered back towards second
Childhood, laughing and gurgling
at practically everything.
And shouted over the heath, "Life is! Life is!
People now smile at me as I pass.
And that is somehow quite nice.

## God Is Wiping His Eyes

Waking from his dreams
God is wiping his eyes,
glancing at me from a corner,
crying for forgiveness.
I can only turn to music,
to the girl in the house of love.
Only she has given me purpose
in this world of endless space,
in this dark of nothingness
where God sang his dirge of death.
So dance! Dance you God!
Destroy! Destroy He cried.
But I create miracles from the girl
with her gift of songs.
Oh hollow God of Holocaust.
No more! No more
will you lick your lips.
No more will you burn my eyes.

# Lost Playgrounds

This afternoon, deep down
in the lost playgrounds of my mind
I sighed.
My young self was running away
from me.
"Hey! Wait! Wait for me." I cried.
Then turned my head and laughed
and laughed at me.
The old man left behind.

# Monolith

My mother was my monolith,
huddling her children close
for the warmth of her belly,
dreaming of better things
for the tomorrow that never came.
A prisoner of poverty,
scanning the sky
Looking through the railings
all the way from Tower Bridge
to Battersea Shore.
And the Thames flowing, but always there.
I watched her smiling,
as she brushed dad aside "Look! My darlings!
Tower Bridge!" Her arms opening,
welcoming all the outcasts of Europe,
desperate to be free.
"Nothing up there!" My dad would cry.
"Wot you looking for? Golden coins
pelting from the sky?"
He turned to the wall and sighed,
and died; and died so many times.
She shook her head and shouted through the railings.
"At least we have our kids and pea soup tonight!"
"Pea soup every night." We all cried.

"Something will turn up. One day." She mumbled.
"You'll see."
Then she would scratch her head and go inside
To sit and stare and stare into space.

One day I remember dad said, come for a walk.
He took me to the other side, where we stood
before four belching monoliths.
In a hushed voice, like being in synagogue,
with his eyes alight, he whispered:
"This is Battersea Power Station."
He was so proud and now shouted aloud:
"Isn't this all wonderful?"
I pinched my nose, wanting to be sick.
Four giant chimneys belching out,
swirling, stinking, yellow clouds of dog-fart.
We hurried home not speaking.
My mother also stank. Just a little, but I loved her.
She hugged me and hugged me into her smell.
My mother! My monolith! Such power! Such fury!
Later I climbed into my buggy bed
and dreamed and dreamed that soon
I would leave this Stepney Green
and fly around the world in my Auto Gyro.
Monolith! Monolith! Great Monoliths attract.
All this was mine. Stonehenge! St Pauls! Notre Dame!

Monoliths tell you that life is forever.
And all these worshippers reaching the sky,
knowing these Gods, these monoliths,
gasping and grunting will always stink
and mystify.
And like my mother they will never die.
You stand before them knowing they will never
move away. They are here to stay.
The Statue of Liberty! The Taj Mahal! Eiffel Tower!
The Pyramids! They bring us together
in endless wonder and worship to the mother God.
And the Great Wall of China!
Tower Bridge! Battersea Power Station!
Of thee I sing!
And the river flows on.

# Oh! The Heat of Your Body

Oh! The heat of your body
late last night,
that brought me to the frontier of tears
and laughter.
You had gone in before me
and I crept in soon after midnight.
Smiling, you turned over in your sleep.
Your mumbled words seemed to say
come to bed.
You had pulled back just one corner of the duvet
for me to slide in beside you.
And climbing into the sea,
I locked my body into yours
and felt the warmth that welded us.
We sailed the singing waves of night
assuring me of dreams forever.

# Oh! Eternal Desire

Out of the dark,
Every night in her silk kimono,
Erica awakes and becomes Salome.
Her humming becomes tabla and flute
and her years fall away
as she smiles and dances in the bedroom.
Soon I jump out of sleep.
Though really far too old for this,
I am compelled to join her.
Slowly at first, my hands waving high
above my head and my feet stamping.
Thumping and thumping.
Now my years fall apart. I dance and dance
as she moves around me. My heart beating,
faster and faster.
Around and around and around I whirl.
And the dream goes on and on.
Until I wake in the morning.

## Waking After Death

So I died.
This is a wild song of my resurrection.
Of a man who loved life
and stumbled through the dark corridors,
looking for God. He was either in the attic
or the basement. He was always somewhere else.
As usual he was not on duty that night.
So I covered myself with sleep.
A million years might have passed,
or seconds. And someone was singing.
It was my wife washing her hair.
Then there was music and
the almond smell of mimosa.

## Eternal Spring

*For Erica on her Birthday*

Throughout the being, the living and
the dying, I looked for you, everywhere.
But never found you. And I was nowhere.
The endless not knowing.
Not caring. Winter and spring, autumn and
summer, and no one to know. Nothing to know.
Who they are, and why and where they are.
The same old afternoon.
Again and again. The yawning desperation.
Waiting, wanting to shut up shop. No one cares.
Neither do I. And the nights.
Inprisoned and poisoned within myself.
But then ... you came down the stairs.
And changed the world. My world. And the world.
And on the darkest winters of my days
you came, opening the door for my life to start.
And your face with your quiet calm was a psalm
when your embrace awoke the engine of my heart.
And the shattering sun exploded, piercing
the bricks in my head. So now darling! Ahead! Ahead!
Now and forever I would never again be dead.
And so we swam and melted into each other.

So soon the path of life was straight ahead.
Come wind, come weather.
And love and desire were the drums
and the guitars our dance of all our nights
and days forever. And all our days are
birthdays.
And all our children come, and our children's
children come and grow with laughter,
in summer, winter, autumn and spring.
And the fulcrum of our love is everything.

## Love, Death and Other Joys

I am approaching the Golden Road to Samarkand,
and I will find you there
with all your love, laughter and joy.
And the songs coming from you.
Though all our years have crumpled into yesterday.
But dreams, laughter I still desire.
My wife. Erica! Eroica! Eureka! Eurydice!
The mistress of truth. Strength. The mother of love.
She is the divine fruit. She is Peaches.
She is Pomegranate. She is Apricots.
But here I must stop for a while, breathe
and sleep; seeking for the lost dreams.
A beautiful repose. Not sleep, but a soft gentle schluff.
Here in the everlasting afternoon,
in this silent, enfolding world,
somewhere in the universe of nothingness.
But we will go soon, so soon.
How swift my tears come, when I swim deep
into the steep river of ravenous death.
And even there I will gladly drown to find you.
Come on! Come on. She shouts.
Into the kitchen where we will make strudel.
From strudel to gornicht, I cry. I moan.
Shtumm! She cries. She sighs. Be a good boy.

My lover. Lazarus! Lazarus!

If you sleep in the day you will die.

Do you hear me? She shouts.

Then tries to pull me out and into the kitchen.

Strudel saves the world.

She murmurs quietly to herself lost songs.

Do you remember the essentials? Come then. There! Here!
Apples! Sugar! Flaked Almonds! Raisins! Cinnamon! Puff
Pastry!

Come! Let's try.

My God! My Goddess! There she is above me. Look!

Her limbs, her lips are spun of silk.

and she is here by the fragrance of her body.

Then she pulls and tugs me, out of my dark
and into the world.

Crying gently punching me
and then comes that kiss, that touch of silk.

And if we were younger both would fall backward into
bed.

Look! She cries. The sun is shining above the garden
of our lives.

She pulls me to kitchen. Work! Work! Move yourself.

Open your brain. Work! Work! Again! And again.

I am dead. I am dead. I groan. Leave me alone.

I want to sleep. I want to stay asleep.

But I don't want to be alone.

Man! Madman of my life, she laughs.
You will have enough sleep. Soon enough.
We will make the cake and you will come alive.
Music! Music! I am swimming in music. Klezmer!
I dance. Gopak! Music! Life! Kazatzka! Hora!
Dance before the death of the world.
I grab her, I shout. We dance.
Then slowly they appear. They creep. I turn cold.
Grandfathers. Great Grandmothers. From all directions.
Great uncles. Great-great uncles. Lost zombie cousins
in stinking mouldy rags, crawling out
from the aeons of the death lands.
Some come from madness into furnace.
Some die of life. How nice. A sweet normal death.
Look! My mishbocher barely move, Watch!
Their masks, a No play, seeing no one,
embracing nothing, nowhere.
They whirl, skulls laughing and laugh on this holiday.
Screeching. Shoving strudel into their mouths.
Look! They're stuffing it down. They are as mad
as drunken wolves. Biting.
Their bones falling apart pounding the floor.
And all their skin falls away.
"Mazeltov!" They shout and slowly start to scream
and crumble. And the grease dissolves,
flames surround, all around them.

Darling! They stink. They smell fog of stench,
the burning meat. Whoosh! They are gone.
I am still dreaming. I do not cry. I am beyond tears.
I am back in the bed of dreams. I must find love.
My love. Her breasts. They make me rest.
They give me breath. And slowly I fly,
gliding down into the garden of joy.
The trees waving and waving, and music, calling me.
The little children rush towards me,
laugh and dance around me.
And I, the tired, collapsing, ragged relic of time,
dance with them as they sing me goodbye!
Goodbye! And hear the Zohar singing.
The world exists by the breath of little children.
So I go down and down on this slide of life.
To find myself approaching the Golden Road of
Samarkand.
But darling, if I do not find you there I shall wait.
And you will arrive. The joy! The Joy of being!
I laugh and laugh and weep for the beauty of life
and the living.

*Terminat hora diem. Terminat auctor opus.*
The hour ends the day. The author ends his work.